RTCA Paper No. 289-00/PMC-108

Ultra-Wideband Technology Radio Frequency Interference Effects to GPS and Interference Scenario Development

First Interim Report to Department of Transportation

Prepared By
RTCA Special Committee 159

12 September 2000

TABLE of CONTENTS

RTCA Special Committee 159
First Interim Report to Dept. of Transportation

1.0   Introduction and Background

In October, 1999, at the request of the Department of Transportation (DoT), the RTCA undertook an effort to investigate the radio frequency interference (RFI) environment in the vicinity of the new Global Positioning System (GPS) L5 frequency (1176.45 ± 12 MHz) and determine appropriate receiver susceptibility criteria and related RFI unwanted emission limits for the use with new civil signal. Aviation-related issues were acknowledged to be of primary importance, but the group was encouraged to seek significant involvement and input from non-aviation GPS uses, especially public safety applications (e.g., maritime, E-911, police, fire fighting). By June 2000 the pace had intensified on regulatory and business activities related to ultra-wideband (UWB) transmission technology. As a result the Department of Transportation requested the RTCA enlarge the study to explicitly treat UWB RFI effects and operational scenarios for the GPS L1 frequency (1575.42 ± 12 MHz) as well as L5.

RTCA had completed a similar RFI environment study for the GPS L1 frequency in late 1996 and published the findings in RTCA/DO-235[1]. The methodology for that study will be used again for the L5 study. It is based on the classic "source-path-receiver" analysis method and involves generating or collecting three basic but interrelated elements. They are emission and location data on potential RFI sources, RFI source encounter scenarios to define the path, and a GPS receiver performance model including RFI effects. The receiver model provides the means to determine the impacts of various interference types in the environment on particular receiver performance parameters. The scenarios are based on particular receiver applications that dictate such things as key receiver performance requirements, what RFI source(s) might be present, and encounter geometry (distance between the RFI source and aircraft GPS antennas). The RFI source data indicate transmitter location and antenna characteristics (for the scenario) and emission types and frequencies (for consideration in the receiver model).

Once the three basic elements had been generated, the final radio frequency (RF) link analyses are performed. The link analysis could yield different outputs depending on the constraints for the particular scenario. A DO-235 example output from the Mobile Satellite Service (MSS) handheld terminal link analysis was the –70 dBW/MHz limit derived for broadband unwanted emissions. In other scenarios, it was the minimum acceptable separation distance to the RFI source.

Sections 2 and 3 to follow discuss the test plans for use in receiver RFI model development and the scenario development, respectively, that the study group has completed as of early August 2000. Section 4 presents a summary and outlines the remaining work.

---

[1] RTCA SC-159, "Assessment of Radio Frequency Interference Relevant to the GNSS," Doc. No. RTCA/DO-235, Jan. 27, 1997, RTCA, Inc., Washington, DC

2.0 UWB RFI Test Plans and RFI Effects Data

The GPS/Wide-Area Augmentation System (WAAS) L1 receiver model[2] was developed to handle CW, broadband noise, and relatively long RF pulsewidth interference sources that represented the L1 RFI environment at the time of the DO-235 study. UWB RFI is a potentially new type that does not fit entirely into one of those categories. Recent preliminary investigations have suggested that some UWB waveforms may have an RFI effect on GPS receivers similar to broadband noise, while other waveforms would be like pulsed or CW RFI. Before a rule making to authorize unlicensed Part 15 UWB operation, it is critically important to test these predictions on a wide range of GPS and other sensitive receivers.

Four test plans were briefed to the RTCA study group and discussed. The following subsections contain summaries of the briefings together with comments, responses, and clarifications that were brought to the group. Preliminary RFI effects data from the Stanford University test program was briefed and is summarized below. Also described is an initial approach developed within the group for application of that data in some key scenarios.

2.1 Stanford University – Department of Transportation Sponsored Tests

2.1.1 Stanford Test Plan and Comments

UWB RFI effects data on GPS receivers are needed to support the analyses of many operational scenarios involving a wide range of potential UWB emissions with or without other interference sources. Thus the two major objectives of the Stanford test are to:
1) quantify the equivalence of UWB RFI to random noise in terms of RFI effect on GPS receivers, and
2) quantify the sensitivity to a wide range of UWB signal parameters in an attempt to span the space of anticipated parameters of commercial units.

The test approach will utilize a single-channel GPS satellite simulator for controlled and repeatable tests. The receiver interference performance test criteria are accuracy for aviation receivers (LAAS requirement of 15 cm smoothed pseudorange standard deviation[3]) and reacquisition time for land receivers (operational E-911 requirement of 1 sec). The candidate aviation precision approach receivers should have interference performance at least to RTCA/DO-229B or DO-253 Minimum Operational Performance Standards (MOPS). A normalization procedure has been included to account for the possibility that the receivers under test may have performance exceeding MOPS requirements by varying amounts.

The rationale for the objective to quantify the degree of equivalence in RFI impact of UWB signals relative to broadband random noise is that the GPS impact and analysis method for broadband noise are reasonably well understood. In this plan, broadband random noise will refer to continuous noise from a noise diode that has power spectral density much broader than the RF/IF bandwidth of the GPS receiver. Such noise is used to model thermal noise in the receiver, sky noise and any other wideband interference sources *other than* UWB. UWB signals (Fig. 1a) also have bandwidths (Fig. 1b) that are greater than the front end of the GPS receiver, but they

---

[2] See RTCA/DO-235 App. C, D, and G
[3] RTCA SC-159, "Minimum Operational Performance Standards for GPS Local Area Augmentation System Airborne Equipment," Doc. No. RTCA/DO-253, Jan. 11, 2000, sec. 2.3.6.8.1 b), RTCA, Inc., Washington, DC

have an additional structure that may cause their RFI effect to be very different that of broadband random noise.

If the degree of RFI impact equivalence were known, that information would directly support the analysis of specific operational interference encounters (scenarios) with or without other interference sources. Such scenarios include aircraft landing (used with MSS, important for WAAS/LAAS), airport surface movement (runway incursion and ramp collision prevention), on-aircraft UWB local area network (LAN), Enhanced-911 land use, etc. The test plan does not, however, include evaluation of specific scenarios and associated link budgets, but only the collection of UWB RFI equivalence data.

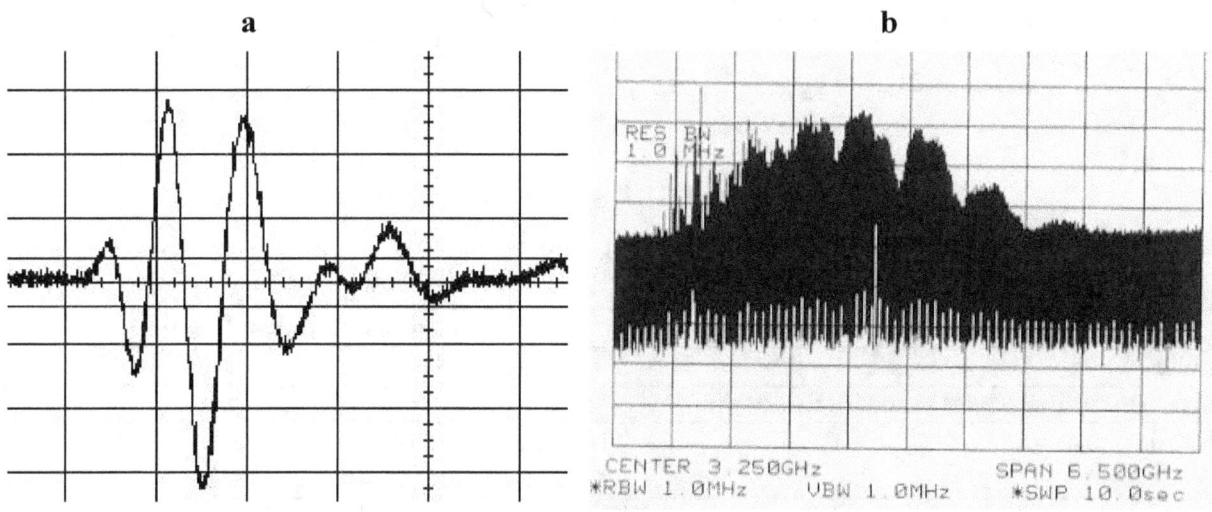

a **b**

Figure 1a. UWB Pulse Time Waveform (0.5 nsec/div)
1b. UWB Pulse Frequency Spectrum (0.65 GHz/div)

The rationale for the second objective is that UWB signals vary greatly and the GPS interference effect is likely sensitive to those variations. For example, Figure 2 depicts a postulated sensitivity to UWB pulse repetition frequency. Tests will determine equivalence as a function of a wide range of UWB signal parameters intended to encompass commercially significant values. Table 1 lists the initial set of parameters; modifications may be made depending early test results. Figures 3-4 illustrate some of the signal waveform variations.

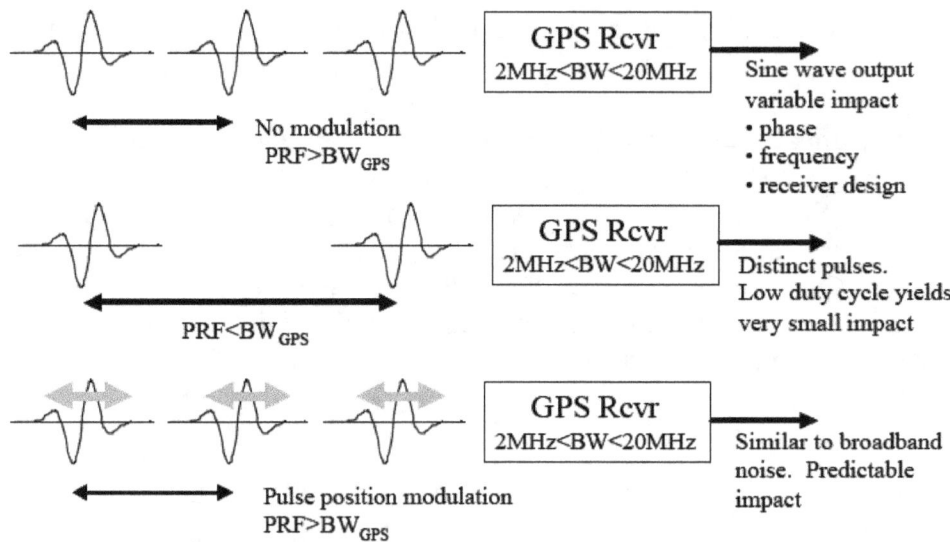

Figure 2. Postulated GPS Sensitivity to UWB PRF

Table 1. Proposed UWB Emission Test Parameters

UWB Emission Parameter	Proposed Value Range
Power	as needed to produce the RFI effect
Pulse Repetition Frequency (PRF) (Mpps)	0.1, 1.0, 20.0
Modulation	None, random on-off-keying (OOK), random pulse position modulation (PPM)
Burst Duty Cycle	10, 50, 100 %
Burst On-Time (millisecond)	0.1, 1 10 msec

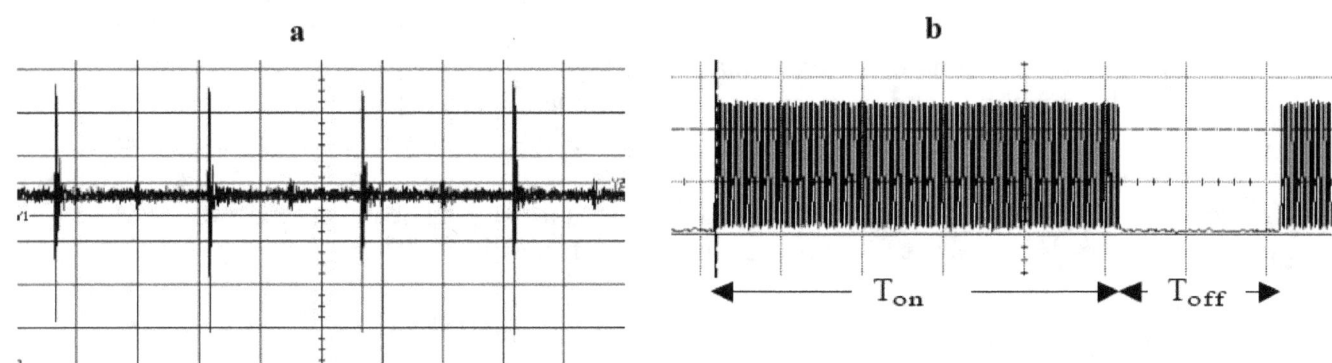

**Figure 3a. Periodic Train of UWB Pulses
3b. Gated Burst of Periodic UWB Pulses**

No Modulation

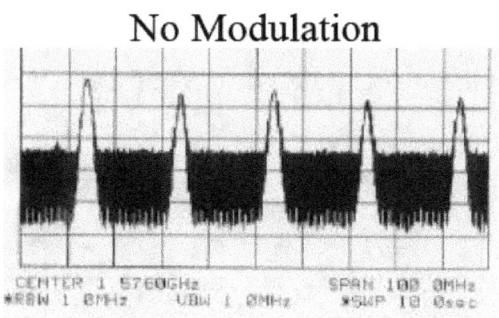

Spectrum With Dithering

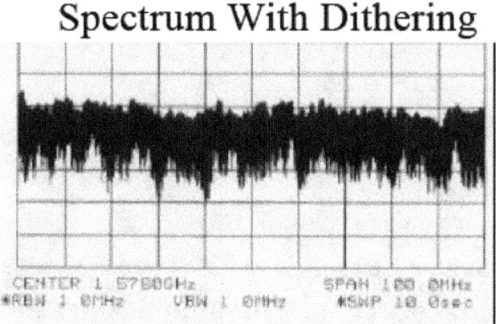

Spectrum of Random OOK

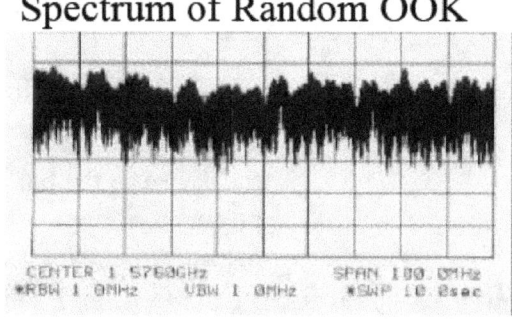

Figure 4. Frequency Spectrum Near GPS L1 for 3 Types of UWB Pulse Modulation

Important dependencies must be understood to enable development of a good GPS receiver RFI model for application to the wide range of GPS scenarios that might contain UWB interference. Existence of a single non-interfering UWB signal should not be sufficient evidence to allow an entire class of new signals.

Besides providing a well-understood performance comparison baseline with UWB RFI, the use of broadband noise also serves to normalize the actual test receiver's performance to that of a minimum performance (MOPS) receiver. The theoretical predicted performance curve (Fig. 5) shows approximately a square root dependence of pseudorange standard deviation (accuracy) with increasing broadband noise power. For operation sufficiently below the loss-of-lock point, performance factors within receivers should cause the curve to translate right or left but not change the basic shape. For a given receiver once the noise power N_{acc} associated with the accuracy limit has been found it serves as the reference point for the remainder of the tests.

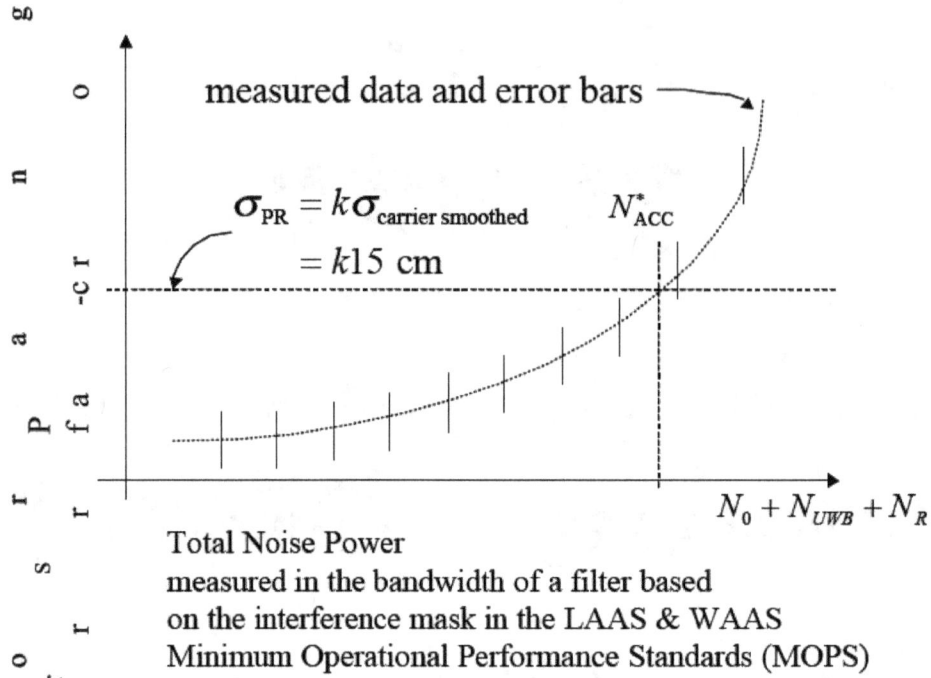

Figure 5. Theoretical Unsmoothed Pseudorange Accuracy vs. Broadband Noise Power

Since it is important to check the scaling of accuracy with interference especially in the case of composite UWB and broadband noise, the test plan calls for using 2 different reduced noise starting values: N_{acc} –4 dB (40% noise and 60% UWB in terms of RFI effect), and N_{acc} –2 dB (63% noise and 37% UWB in terms of RFI effect). With UWB power as the independent variable, a wide range of UWB waveform parameter sets can be checked for RFI effect relative to broadband noise. Two cases are illustrated in Figure 6: one where the UWB waveform has less RFI for a given power, and one where the RFI effect is greater than broadband noise. In each case a noise-equivalent correction factor can be read from the curve.

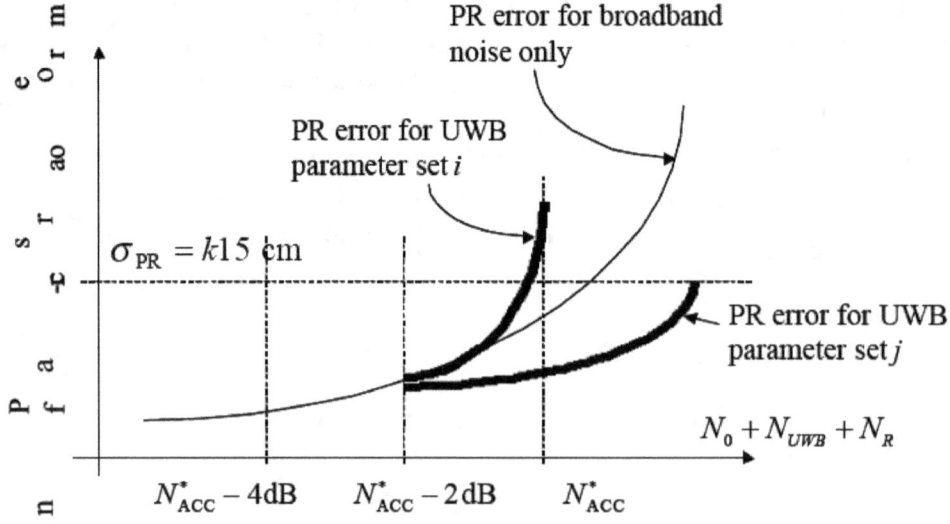

Note: error bars have been suppressed in this figure.

Figure 6. Illustration of UWB-Noise Equivalence (UWB added to broadband noise)

The Stanford Test Plan was favorably received by the RTCA study group after a few minor clarifications. The plan was also reviewed and coordinated through the government Interdepartment Radio Advisory Committee and put out for public comment via a Federal Register Notice. Comments from Time Domain Corporation were received by DoT and brought to the RTCA study group at its August meeting. Because of a shortage of time the study group was unable to discuss the comments.

2.1.2   Stanford Test Preliminary Results

Preliminary UWB RFI test data from the Stanford University tests were presented to the RTCA study group at its August 2000 meeting. The data covered the effects of one UWB source on one GPS receiver with performance typical of an aviation precision approach GPS receiver and included different UWB PRFs (100 kpps-20 Mpps), different burst duty cycles (10%-100%), different burst on-time (10us-10ms), and two types of pulse modulation (no modulation and random PPM). Initial test procedure validation results show 1 dB steps of attenuation of the broadband noise source are definitely distinguishable. The correspondence factor (k) between unsmoothed pseudorange standard deviation (the actual measured parameter) and 100-second smoothed value (15 cm requirement) was established empirically (k=9.333). Thus the unsmoothed value corresponding to the 15 cm requirement was found to be 1.4 meters. The purpose of using "raw" measurements instead of smoothed measurements was to minimize test time. The empirically established value of "k" agreed well with theory. Total average interference power (broadband noise plus UWB, if present) was measured at the output of a 20 MHz wide bandpass RF filter connected to the receiver's input terminal. A 60 minute run time (3600 independent samples) was chosen to yield ±2.4% measurement uncertainty at a 95% confidence level. The GPS signal power was set to -131dBm (3.5 dB above minimum spec.) for test convenience and the receiver normalization test against broadband noise was run. The GPS generator setting for subsequent tests was held at –131 dBm.

The normalization data (Fig. 7) show that the 1.4 m unsmoothed pseudorange standard deviation limit was reached at a noise input power of –89 dBm (better than minimum performance when adjusted for the stronger GPS signal). The receiver lost GPS signal lock at a noise input 4 dB above the input where the accuracy limit was reached.

9

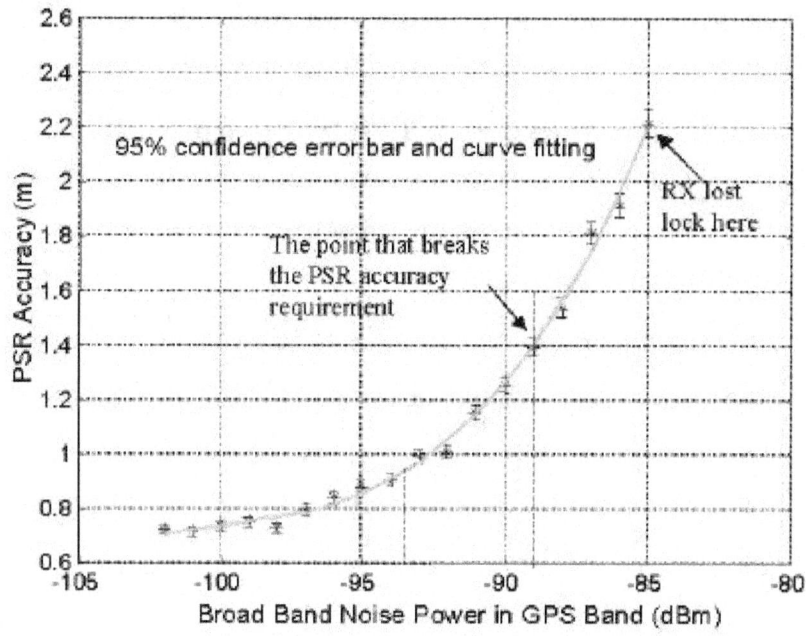

Figure 7. Receiver Normalization – Pseudorange Accuracy vs. Broadband Noise Power

Note: Based on variance measurements from raw PSR and from 100-sec carrier smoothed PSR, 1.4 m of unsmoothed PSR accuracy (Fig. 7 vert. axis) was found equivalent to the 15 cm carrier-smoothed PSR accuracy requirement.

The broadband noise input power was reduced 4 dB to a setting of about –93.5 dBm and a UWB signal with several different combinations of UWB waveform parameters was combined with the reduced noise. UWB power was increased in 1 dB steps until the accuracy degraded beyond the limit or receiver loss-of-lock occurred. In each case to follow the broadband noise curve is plotted for reference and all responses are plotted against the total interference power (UWB + broadband noise) in the GPS band. Figure 8 shows the comparison of the noise RFI effect with that of various UWB PRF values with 100 % duty cycle (no pulse burst) and no other pulse modulation. Note that for PRF values below 1 MHz, the RFI effect is reduced but for values of 5, 10, and 20 MHz the curves fall on the noise curve (labeled "RF Only"). One exception is the curve for a 19.94 MHz PRF. In this case the receiver lost lock with only a negligible increase in total power from UWB above the reduced noise starting point. Note also that the break-lock accuracy values for UWB and broadband noise were rather closer to the required accuracy limit than for broadband noise alone.

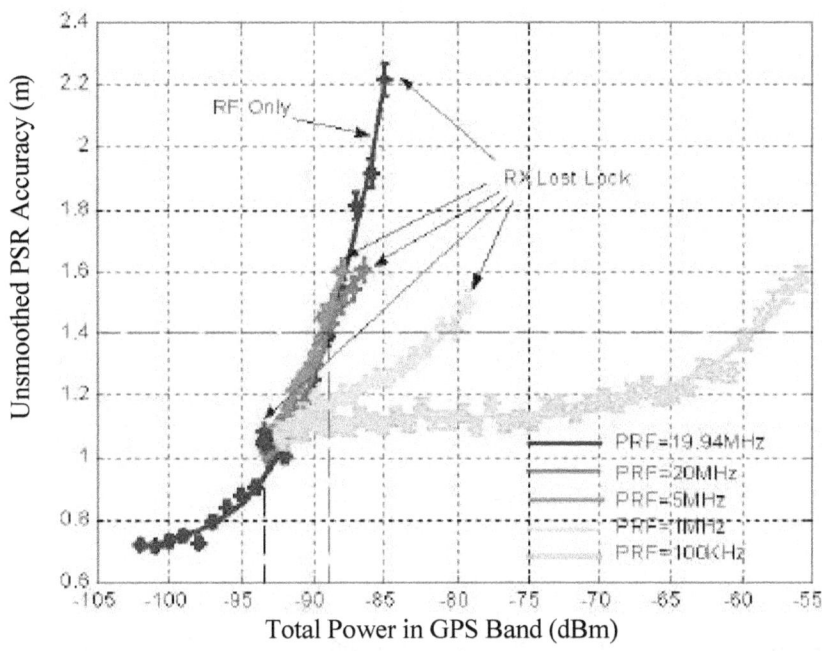

Figure 8. Comparison of PRF Effects (100%Duty Cycle, No Modulation)

The details of the sensitive spectral line frequency effect were explored by slightly varying the PRF and monitoring the UWB line spectrum near 1575.42 MHz (the GPS L1 carrier). Effects at three different PRF values near 20 MHz illustrate the susceptibility when the RFI spectral lines overlap with GPS L1 C/A code spectral lines. Figures 9 and 10 show the pseudorange accuracy and loss-of-lock characteristics and line spectra, respectively.

Results on the effects of UWB pulse train burst duty cycle (Fig. 11) show reduced RFI impact compared to broadband noise for 20 MHz PRF and duty cycles as low as 10%. The effect rises sharply above 10% such that the 50% and 100% curves overlay the noise-only curve. Reducing the duty cycle from 100% to 10% does not reduce the RFI impact, however, in the 19.94 MHz PRF case (recall the spectral line effect).

Results on the UWB burst on-time effects at 50% duty cycle (Fig. 12) show little change at 20 MHz PRF over the noise-only case until the on-time is greater than 1 millisecond. Even then the total power to exceed the accuracy limit is only about 2 dB more than the noise-only case. The 10 microsecond on-time curve at 19.94 MHz PRF shows very slight reduction in impact compared to the 100% duty cycle case.

11

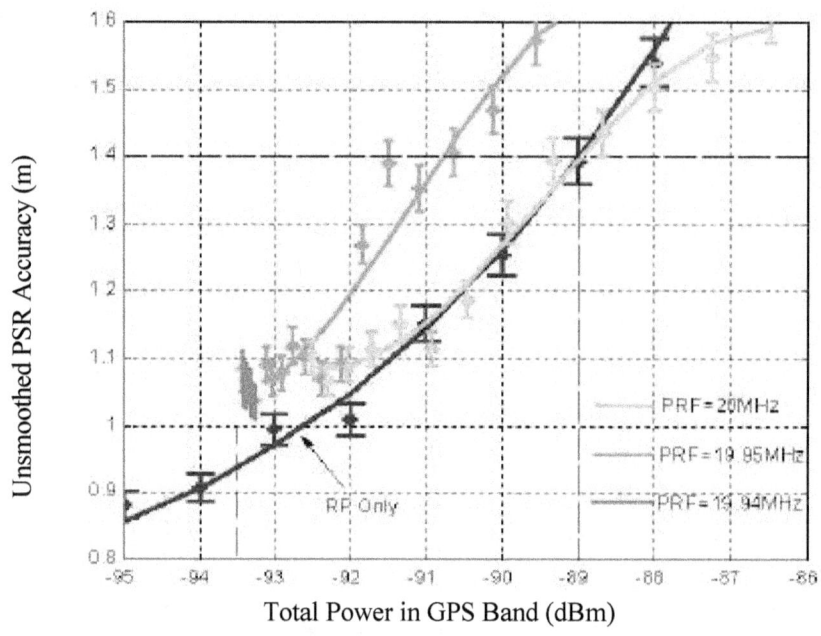

Figure 9. Spectrum Line Sensitivity (100 % Duty Cycle No Mod.)

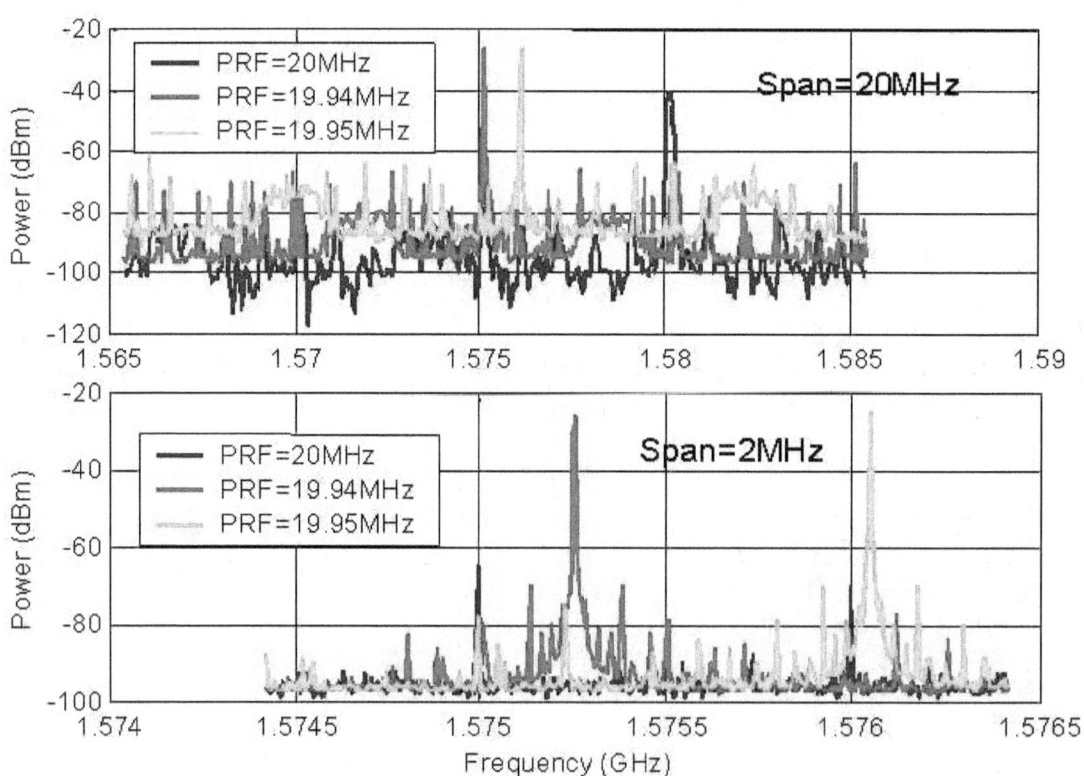

Figure 10. UWB Spectral Lines Near 1575.42 MHz (100% Duty Cycle, No Pulse Mod)

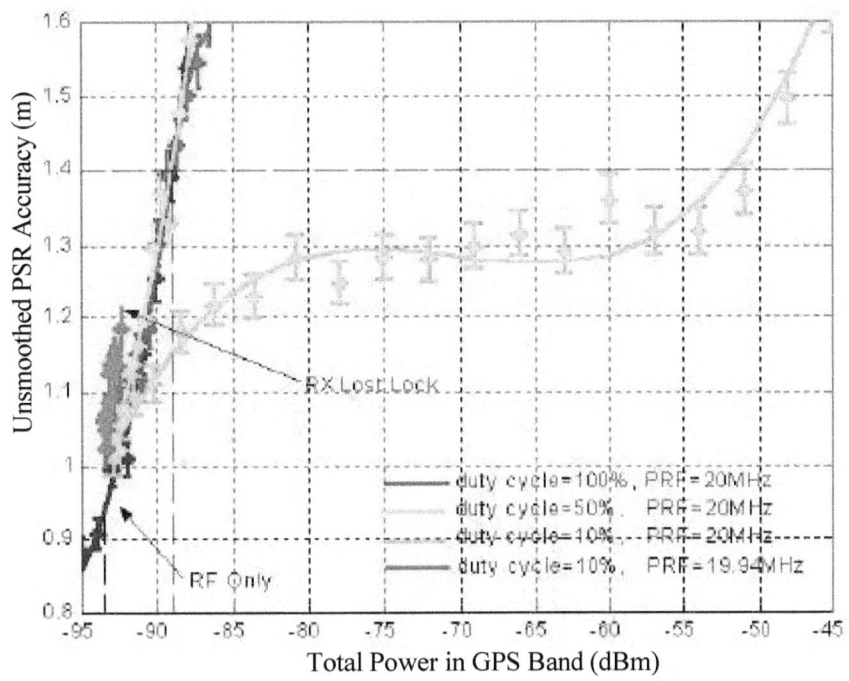

Figure 11. UWB Burst Duty Cycle Effect (PRF near 20 MHz, No Mod.)

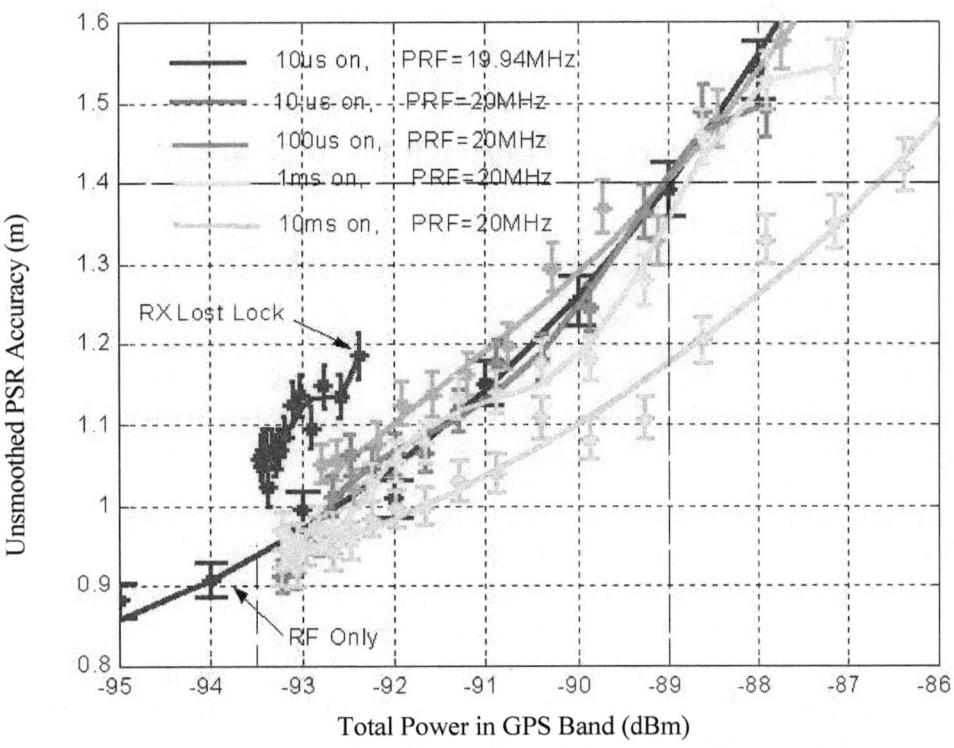

Figure 12. Burst On-Time Effect at 50 % Duty Cycle (PRF near 20 MHz, No Mod.)

Results on the UWB random PPM (or dither) waveform (Fig. 13) show dithering reduces the RFI impact (in total power terms) at 20 MHz PRF about 1.5 dB at the accuracy limit. Dithering also helps to diminish the spectral line sensitivity for 19.94 MHz PRF at least in the sense that loss-of-lock occurred at a higher total power.

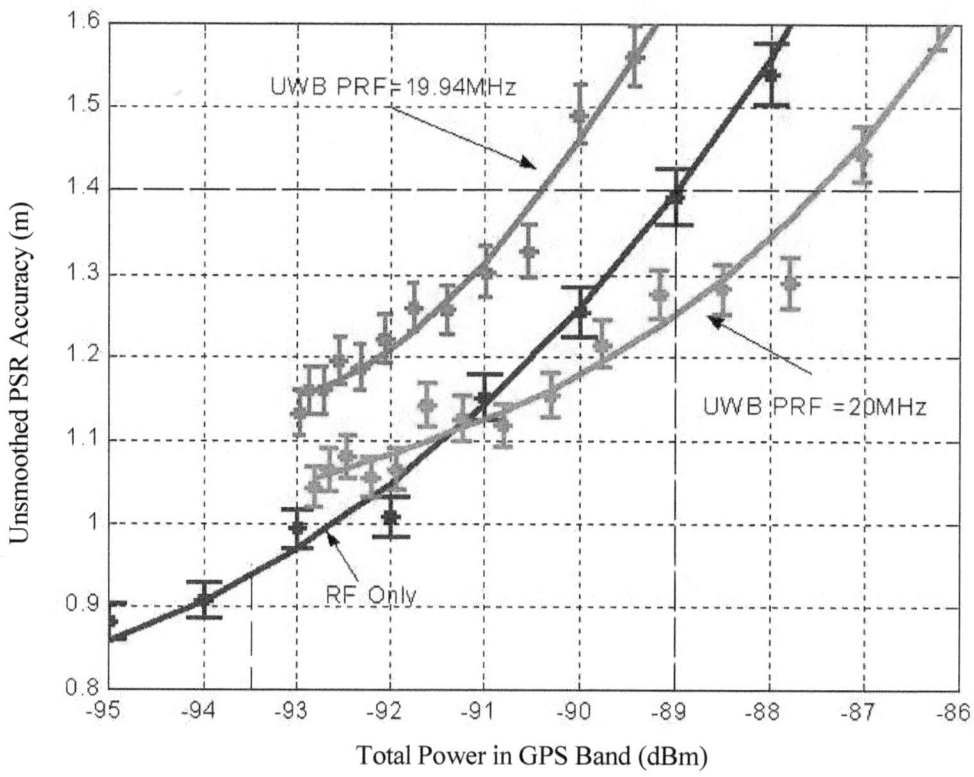

Figure 13. Random Pulse Position Mod. Effect (PRF near 20 MHz, 100% Duty Cycle)

In summary thus far from preliminary data on the first aviation receiver, Stanford results have demonstrated in many respects the expected dependence on UWB parameters. The preliminary data indicates the location of spectral lines relative to GPS C/A code lines is important for all PRFs, duty cycles, on-times & modulation. Lower PRF (relative to receiver bandwidth – thought to approach 20 MHz for the unit tested) has less RFI impact. Lower duty cycle, longer burst on-time, and random PPM (dithering) seem to lessen RFI impact. UWB pulse trains with no modulation have a strong RFI impact.

2.1.3 Preliminary Results Discussion

After some minor clarifications on terminology and test conditions, the study group received the Stanford data quite favorably. There was general agreement on the Stanford's results summary thus far. There was also general agreement that although the data represent a good step forward much more is needed. Stanford needs to complete the remaining 50% of the aviation receiver test matrix and tests on the land GPS receiver. Other tests are needed to cover a wider range of GPS receivers as well as to repeat the Stanford tests on another aviation precision approach receiver. Although the Stanford tests show the effects of a UWB signal aggregated with broadband noise, RFI aggregation effects of multiple UWB signals are also very much needed.

An initial concept was discussed for the use of the Stanford data in the group's RFI study and in recommendations for FCC rule making. The procedure is based on the main outcome of the Stanford tests - a determination of the UWB noise equivalency correction factors for any UWB-device modulation format. If the UWB spectrum is equivalent in RFI effect to the broadband noise, no correction to the UWB source spectrum is necessary. This means that if the power necessary to generate a 15cm error is the same for the UWB-device as it is for a broadband noise source then the UWB source is equivalent to broadband noise. If however the power necessary for the UWB-device to generate a 15cm error is smaller than the broadband noise source, then a negative correction factor (penalty) is necessary to reduce the UWB source power spectrum. On the other hand if the power for the UWB-device is larger than the broadband noise source, then a positive correction factor (credit) is allowed and the UWB source power spectrum can be increased accordingly. From the preliminary test results, it is evident that both cases (penalty and credit) exist.

These correction factors go easily into conventional link budgets derived for any UWB-device in any aeronautical or non-aeronautical GPS scenario. From the link budgets, the GPS protection limit for UWB RFI can be calculated and the emission limit at the UWB source specified. Once sufficient correction factor data are available on a wide enough range of GPS receivers, generalized receiver models with associated susceptibility limits can be used as appropriate for each scenario. Other factors needed are the separation distance between the GPS receiver and the UWB source and the GPS antenna gain toward the source. Since we assume the UWB device always operates in the presence of an MSS MET we also must define the separation distance between the MET and the victim GPS receiver.

To illustrate all the input details of the analysis procedure 3 example scenarios are chosen with a UWB device and an MSS terminal present at various distances. They are the aeronautical services Category I and LAAS Category II operations and E-911 ambulance service. We arbitrarily assume that the noise equivalency correction factors are 0 dB for Category I, +1 dB, for Category II and –2 dB for the E-911 ambulance application. In other words we assume 3 different UWB devices. The receiver interference allowance value for the E-911 case is just an estimate while the Cat I/II values are related to requirements. Table 1 illustrates the link budget methodology. As shown we use an MSS source to GPS victim link budget followed by a UWB protection limit procedure and than a GPS victim to UWB device link budget that gives the final number - the UWB device allowed source emission limit.

For Category II approaches, the antenna separation distance is 70 ft or less; this means that the path loss is –63 dB instead of the –66.1 dB for 100ft separation distance in the Category I approach. We achieve the necessary interference protection limit by reducing the GPS antenna gain in the direction of the RFI from –10 dB to –13.1 dB.

The UWB Notice of Proposed Rule Making (NPRM) suggested that the Part 15 limits should be reduced 12 dB for safety of life applications below 2 GHz. This is consistent with frequency management procedures when there is no margin available in the victim system for out-of-band RFI sources.

Table 2 presents three link budgets for UWB RFI for three GPS scenarios, two aeronautical and one example non-aeronautical scenario. For the Category I application, the UWB must reduce its spectrum in the 1559 to 1610 MHz band by 11dB below the Part 15 limit, and 10 dB for the Category II application. The assumed non-aeronautical GPS scenario places the MSS RFI 70 ft from the victim GPS, and the UWB RFI source 30 ft from the victim GPS. The example susceptibility limit for the non-aeronautical GPS is –138 dBW/MHz. Under the given assumptions, the UWB device RFI must be reduced by 20.4 dB. Note: Applications where separation is less than 30 ft, including cosite applications and E-911 applications, are not covered by this example. Part 15 regulations do not consider RFI scenarios, and simply give an emission limit without regard to compatibility.

Table 2. Example UWB Emission Limit Link Budgets (with Application of Correction Factors)

	GPS WAAS/LAAS Category I	GPS LAAS Category II	GPS Non-aeronautical
MSS RFI Pwr Spect. Density at source	-70 dBW/MHz [1]	-70 dBW/MHz [1]	-70 dBW/MHz[1]
Propag. Loss, (Ant. separation dist.)	-66.1 dB (100ft)	-63.0 dB (70ft)	-63 dB (70 ft)
GPS Antenna Gain toward RFI	-10 dB	-13.1 dB	-5 dB
GPS Allowance for Ext. RFI (MSS RFI is broadband noise)	-146.1dBW/MHz (MSS) -116.1dBm/MHz	-146.1dBW/MHz -116.1dBm/MHz	-138 dBW/MHz -108 dBm/MHz
UWB Noise Equivalent Correction Factor [2]	-0 dB	+1dB	-2dB[4]
NPRM suggested UWB RFI Limit [3] below Part 15	-12 dB	-12 dB	-12 dB
Protection Limit Against UWB	-158.1 dBW/MHz -128.1 dBm /MHz	-157.1 dBW/MHz -127.1 dBm /MHz	-152 dBW/MHz -122 dBm /MHz
GPS Antenna gain correction	10 dB	13.1dB	5dB
Propag. Loss (Ant. separation distance)	66.1 dB (100ft)	63.0 dB (70ft)	55.6(30ft)
Emission Limit at UWB source	-82.0 dBW/MHz -52.0dBm/MHz	-81.0 dBW/MHz -51.0dBm/MHz	-91.4 dBW/MHz -61.4 dBm/MHz
Part 15 Limit	-71 dBW/MHz	-71 dBW/MHz	-71 dBW/MHz
UWB Limit relative to Part 15	-11 dB	-10 dB	-20.4 dB

Note 1: MSS ITU allocation

Note 2: If UWB RFI lies above broadband noise RFI, Correction Factor is negative (debit). If UWB RFI lie below broadband noise RFI, Correction Factor is positive (credit).

Note 3: -12 dB is consistent with International (ITU) Frequency Management Practices when no margin is available and RFI is out-of-band

Note 4: Three different example correction factors have been used for comparison.

2.2 Univ. of Texas Applied Research Labs – Time Domain Corp. Sponsored Tests

2.2.1 University of Texas ARL Test Plan

The objective of the testing described in the ARL:UT test plan is to measure the behavior of GPS receivers in response to UWB emissions in highly controlled environments. From the raw data collected, it should be possible to determine, for separately defined operational scenarios, representative minimum operating distances between representative UWB transmitters, operating in specific modes, and representative GPS receivers, operating in given modes, such that the GPS receivers would experience no harmful interference. Additionally, from the data collected it should be possible to derive potential effects on GPS receivers from aggregation of UWB transmitters in a given locale.

Although some proposed analysis methods are outlined in this test plan, it is not the objective of this project to extensively analyze the data acquired. The analysis discussed in this plan only represents a rationale for why the specific data is to be collected. Neither is it the purpose of this test plan to attempt to predict the impacts of the FCC's NPRM to GPS receivers in any operational scenario. The primary intent of this project and test plan is to acquire data that will allow anyone with the appropriate technical background, and a thorough quantitative understanding of operational scenarios of interest, to estimate the impact of the measured UWB emissions.

This test plan is by no means intended to represent an "end-all" conclusive data acquisition procedure. This test is limited in scope and is a first step in an exploration of the impacts of Ultra Wideband technologies on GPS receivers. The key limitations are:

a) Only a limited number of UWB technologies will be tested. While the UWB emissions to be tested represent the dominant waveforms of interest to the FCC, they do not represent every potential UWB device or technology in existence today.

b) Only a limited number of candidate GPS receivers will be tested. The chosen receivers are intended to be a representative cross-section of modern, good-quality, commercially available GPS receiver technologies. The chosen receivers do not represent the lower quality GPS receivers available in the market today, nor do they currently represent military receivers due to the classified nature of military GPS receivers. The use of classified data would prohibit the publication of the data for public record; therefore military receivers are not currently included in this test plan.

Nevertheless, despite these limitations, ARL:UT strongly believes that this measurement program will allow quantifying the impact of UWB on GPS with sufficient precision to serve as a basis for FCC decision-making.

This GPS susceptibility testing program consists of:

a) conducted tests using a GPS signal simulator (see Figure 14),

b) outdoor radiated tests to ensure there are no systematic errors in the conducted tests, and

c) aggregate tests to assess the effect of multiple UWB emitters in a 'real world' environment.

More details can be found in the test plan posted on the ARL:UT / CURE web site at
http://sgl.arlut.utexas.edu/asd/Cure/testplan.html

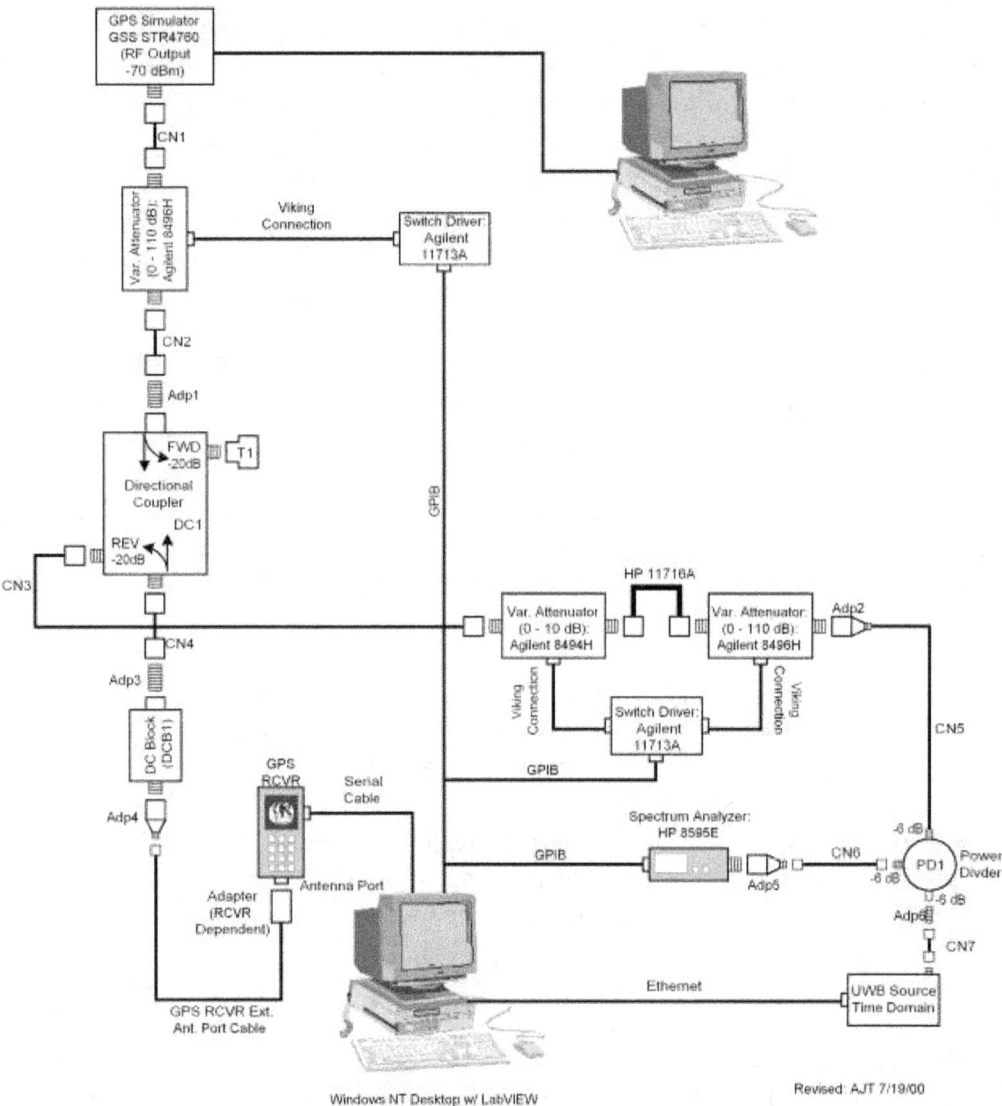

Figure 14. Conducted Test Cable and Connector Laboratory Setup

2.2.2 University of Texas ARL Plan Comments and Clarifications

After the initial presentation of the test plan to the RTCA study group, five significant comments on the approach were made during group discussion. Responses by ARL:UT were offered to the group at a subsequent meeting and, in a few instances, further clarifications requested. These are grouped together with the initial comment.

Comment 1: The tests would be more representative of the real environment if they were done with UWB emissions less than 100% of the budget. Since there is always broadband noise present, some of the budget needs to be made up of broadband noise. By comparison, the DoT-Stanford test plan uses 0%, 37%, and 60 % UWB contributions to the total receiver performance budget.

ARL Response 1: The Stanford requirement for a receiver to be tested in such a manner is derived from RTCA requirements in documents such as RTCA/DO-229B, section 2.5.7. This requirement is aviation-specific and may not be representative of other communities-of-interest's test methodologies. Additionally this method has a built-in assumption that UWB signals have spectral characteristics similar to broadband noise and that the spectral characteristics of UWB signals shall be additive with broadband noise across the GPS bands for all tested UWB signal parameters; i.e., PRF's, burst modes, and duty cycles.

RTCA Reply: ARL:UT made the statement that UWB signals are assumed to be 'white noise' in the Stanford plan. On the contrary, the Stanford plan proposes to relate UWB emissions to a white noise source for the purpose of determining if there is an equivalence between UWB and a white noise source.

Clarification: ARL:UT has re-read the Stanford test plan and recognizes the position Stanford is taking regarding this assumption. It was not clear from an earlier review of the test plan that this was the intent of the Stanford effort. ARL:UT withdraws this comment.

Comment 2: The DoT-Stanford test actually attempts to quantify the correspondence of various UWB waveform interference effect on GPS to that of broadband random noise. The Univ. of Texas ARL test plan does not and that difference will complicate the application of the test results to final UWB regulations.

ARL Response 2: ARL:UT agrees with this concept and has introduced a white noise source into the testing procedures as a "baseline" against which the impacts of UWB signals can be correlated. The methods by which the white noise source shall be utilized will be similar to the manner that Stanford uses in their initial calibration of each receiver to determine the signal level of the white noise source at which the receiver falls outside the 15 cm limit. As opposed to the Stanford test plan, the ARL:UT test plan will then test the impacts of the UWB signal by itself. It is our belief that this will allow for a much easier comparison of the effects of a UWB signal as compared to the white noise source. Also, by testing each signal independently, the effects of the UWB signal on the GPS receiver will not be masked by the white noise source, something that may happen in the Stanford test.

Comment 3: Bench tests should use minimum guaranteed GPS signal strength (-164.5 dBW) and should be conducted with a single simulated GPS signal to minimize unnecessary satellite constellation effects. For aviation receivers the most important performance parameter is pseudorange accuracy. Determination of code-minus-carrier variance essentially eliminates the bias of the simulator.

> ARL Response 3: ARL:UT recognizes that a single channel of information may be sufficient to assess pseudorange accuracy for aviation grade receivers. However, ARL:UT maintains that additional information is required to assess positioning and survey performance, and that collection of additional satellite data in no way prevents an analyst from extracting single channel information. Additionally ARL:UT agrees that minimum GPS signal strengths at the receiver port shall be −136 dBm as identified in RTCA/DO-229B section 2.5.c(2).

Comment 4: Outdoor radiated tests, because they are not worst case, are not controlled, and cannot be reproduced, are of little value in producing data which can be used to set a standard. Outdoor tests should only be done to validate conclusions reached via bench tests. Outdoor testing is also flawed by uncontrolled multipath, which may swamp the results of the UWB RFI. The multipath environment for aviation precision approach is quite different.

> ARL Response 4: ARL:UT recognizes the limitations imposed by radiated testing. The intent was to follow the conducted tests with outdoor radiated tests as a validation of the bench tests (as stated by RTCA). ARL:UT understands that GPS signal multipath may impact the ability to recognize UWB interference. ARL:UT has taken precautions to mitigate the occurrence of GPS signal multipath and will make efforts to quantify the RF environment prior to, during, and following UWB emissions.

Comment 5: Verify that the data taken can be analyzed in such a way to be of value to the aviation community. The lack of post-processing of the raw receiver measurements will likely complicate significantly the analysis of aviation receiver results compared to the Stanford plan.

> ARL Response 5: AR:UT will not take any actions that would violate the integrity of the raw measurement data collected during this effort. ARL:UT maintains that any analyst can duplicate the 'post-processing' that produces the data used for a determination of impact as described in the DoT-Stanford test plan The DoT-Stanford test plan is not acquiring any special data that ARL:UT is not; in fact, ARL:UT is acquiring significantly more data. ARL:UT's role in this effort is limited to data collection and ARL:UT will not perform any data processing or analysis.

> RTCA Reply: ARL:UT should investigate the possibility of performing post-processing similar to Stanford for a trial validation of its own data.

> Clarification: ARL:UT recognizes the value of having a common point of reference between the Stanford effort and our own testing efforts. ARL:UT will seriously consider this recommendation and will attempt to comply provided sufficient funding and time are available within the scope of our current efforts.

Clarification was also requested on how the UWB test pulse characteristics will be captured and documented in the ARL:UT tests.

<u>ARL Response</u>: As stated in the ARL:UT test plan, ARL:UT will characterize the UWB device against the FCC Part 15 requirements in an FCC laboratory and will utilize a spectrum analyzer to collect the following measurements during each test case:

1) UWB spectral content in 2 MHz and 20 MHz bands around both L1 and L2 GPS frequencies,

2) UWB average power in 2 MHz and 20 MHz bands around both L1 and L2 GPS frequencies, and 3) UWB instantaneous power 2 MHz and 20 MHz bands around both L1 and L2 GPS frequencies.

In addition, ARL:UT will utilize a high speed digital sampling oscilloscope to characterize the peak pulse power and waveform shape for each operational mode to be tested. Finally, ARL:UT will utilize a power meter and power sensor to characterize the average power for each test mode. These measurements will be incorporated into the final test plan to be issued after completion of the data collection campaign.

In the initial discussion it was noted that the DoT-Stanford plan was undergoing review and coordination through the IRAC. Plans that deviate from that are not viewed favorably by FAA and DoD GPS-Joint Program Office. UT:ARL responded that they have contacted the IRAC and are awaiting comment. Efforts to present the ARL:UT test plan to the FAA and the GPS-JPO were made in good faith, in an effort to develop a test plan that would best serve the community. The RTCA study group was subsequently informed that the GPS-JPO did provide comments to ARL:UT on the plan but the study group did not review those comments.

2.3 NTIA/NIST Tests

2.3.1 UWB Characterization and Assessment of Impact to Government Radio Systems (excluding GPS)

Because of its responsibility for managing the Federal Government's use of the RF spectrum, the National Telecommunications and Information Administration (NTIA) has developed a comprehensive program to study the potential effects of UWB emissions to critical Federal radio frequency systems. The key elements of the NTIA study program include laboratory measurements, analysis, computer simulation, and documentation in the form of both a response to the NPRM and a final report. The results of the laboratory measurements will feed into the analysis and computer simulation efforts in order to predict the impact of UWB signals on critical federal government radio frequency systems. Three organizations are collaborating in the study: the NTIA Office of Spectrum Management (OSM), the NTIA Institute for Telecommunication Sciences (ITS), and the National Institute of Science and Technology (NIST).

The primary objectives of the effort are to:

a) develop measurement procedures to characterize UWB emissions using commercial-off-the-shelf measurement equipment,

b) determine the susceptibility of selected radio receivers by observing the effects of UWB signals in their receiver IF sections,

c) develop one-on-one interference analysis procedures,

d) validate the one-on-one interference analysis procedures with field measurements of selected Federal radio receivers, and

e) demonstrate how multiple UWB emissions add within a receiver.

The master plan[4] and the measurement plan[5] that describe this measurement effort can be found on the worldwide web at http://www.ntia.doc.gov/osmhome/uwbtestplan.

The candidate Federal systems to be considered in this measurement effort are listed below (Table 3). GPS is deliberately omitted since it is the subject of a separate effort described in Section 2.3.2. The measurements are currently being conducted at the ITS and NIST laboratories in Boulder, CO.

Table 3. Candidate Federal Systems to be Considered.

SYSTEM	FREQUENCY BAND OF OPERATION
Instrument Landing System	108-112 and 328.6-335.4 MHz
Distance Measuring Equipment	960-1215 MHz
Air Traffic Control Radio Beacon	1030 and 1090 MHz
Air Route Surveillance Radar	1215-1400 MHz
SARSAT Receivers	1544.5 MHz
Fixed Microwave System	1755-1850 MHz
Airport Surveillance Radar	2700-2900 MHz
Earth Station Receiver	3700-4200 MHz
Radar Altimeters	4200-4400 MHz
Microwave Landing System	5030-5090 MHz
Terminal Doppler Weather Radar	5600-5650 MHz

2.3.2 Measurement Effort to Assess the Potential Interference Impact from UWB Transmission Systems to GPS Receivers.

The Interagency GPS Executive Board (IGEB) Senior Steering Group (SSG) approved funding to NTIA in late June for a measurement effort to assess the potential interference impact to GPS receivers from UWB emissions. Shortly thereafter, NTIA developed a program plan to assess the electromagnetic compatibility of UWB transmitters and GPS receivers. The key elements of this program are a measurement effort, an analysis effort, and a documentation effort.

The measurement effort of this program involves the development of a measurement plan, the acquisition of the necessary measurement hardware, the development of a measurement system, and the collection and reduction of the measurement data. NTIA OSM and NTIA ITS have collaborated to develop a measurement plan[6] that will be implemented by ITS. This

---

[4] NTIA, Ultra-Wideband Signals for Sensing and Communication: A Master Plan for Developing Measurement Methods, Characterizing the Signals and Estimating Their Effects on Existing Systems, June 15, 2000.

[5] NTIA, Ultra-Wideband Signals for Sensing and Communication: A Master Plan for Developing Measurement Methods, Characterizing the Signals and Estimating Their Effects on Existing Systems, ITS Ultra-Wideband Measurement Plan, (Master Plan Task 1.2), June 14, 2000.

[6] NTIA, Measurement Plan to Determine the Potential Interference Impact to Global Positioning System Receivers from Ultra-wideband Transmission Systems, August 8, 2000.

measurement plan establishes tasks to be performed that will relate UWB signal characteristics to GPS performance criterion. These tasks include:

a) identification of GPS receivers to be considered;

b) identification of UWB signal parameters to be considered;

c) development of the GPS/UWB measurement methodology;

d) development of measurement procedures to assess the potential for single source UWB interference;

e) development of measurement procedures to assess the potential for aggregate UWB interference; and

f) data recording and reporting methods.

More information about this measurement effort, including the full plan text, can be found on the worldwide web at http://www.ntia.doc.gov/osmhome/uwbtestplan/gpstestfr.htm.

The DoT-sponsored study at Stanford University, previously described, is already underway to assess the potential impact from UWB devices an aviation precision approach GPS receiver and a public safety land GPS receiver. To supplement rather than duplicate this effort, the NTIA plan will consider GPS receivers used in other applications. Table 4 has a candidate list. Note that the aviation receivers in Table 4 are TSO C129 types generally used for enroute navigation (less stringent accuracy) whereas the DoT-Stanford tests involve precision approach-capable receivers.

TABLE 4: Candidate GPS Test Receivers.

APPLICATION	GPS RECEIVER	TECHNOLOGY EMPLOYED
Aviation[7]	Trimble 8100	code tracking
	Canadian Marconi CMA-900	code tracking
	Garmin GPS-155XL	code tracking
Maritime	Trimble NT300D	code tracking; DGPS capable
	Garmin GPSMAP-215	code tracking; DGPS capable
	NovAtel Performance	code & carrier tracking; narrow correlator spacing
Public Safety	Trimble ACE Board	code tracking
	Garmin GPS-25 Board	code tracking
Surveying	NovAtel OEM4-RT-20	code & carrier tracking; narrow correlator spacing
	Ashtech Z-Surveyor	code & carrier tracking; cross-correlator
	Allen Osborne Associates, Inc SNR-8000	code (C/A and P) tracking; cross-correlator
	Trimble 4000 SSI	code & carrier tracking, cross-correlator, narrow correlator spacing
Agriculture/Mining	Trimble AG-132	code & carrier tracking
Timing	Motorola UT Plus Oncore	code & carrier tracking

The immediate problem encountered in developing a plan to assess the impact of UWB to the GPS receivers considered in this plan was that performance metrics and criteria are not well defined for these GPS applications. Therefore, for this effort, the metric proposed for assessing interference is receiver break-lock, i.e., the level of interference that will cause the loss of the desired GPS signal to a GPS receiver. Since a break lock condition represents the ultimate interference to a GPS receiver, the actual interference criterion must be set at a level somewhat less than the break lock level. In this plan, a level of 2 dB below the break lock level is proposed as an initial criterion, provided that reacquisition of the GPS satellite is unencumbered. Pseudo range error will be monitored to ensure against discontinuities while the interfering signal is increased to the break-lock level.

One critical assumption that is made in the proposed measurement plan is the initial condition assumed for the GPS receiver. Under actual operational conditions, i.e., outside of a laboratory setting, a GPS receiver is subjected to additional noise that is introduced by the environment in which it operates. Factors such as sky noise, cross-correlation noise introduced from satellites in the GPS constellation other than the one being tracked, and noise resulting from GPS

---

[7] Department of Transportation, Federal Aviation Administration, Technical Standard Order C-129a, Airborne Supplemental Navigation Equipment Using the Global Positioning System (GPS).

augmentation systems and other radionavigation systems presently operating or proposed for operation in the band, will be accounted for by adding the UWB signal to an initial level of broadband noise. Since it is difficult, if not impossible to estimate the levels of each individual contributor to this broadband noise, the initial level will be determined based on the minimum guaranteed GPS signal power of -130 dBm into a 0 dBi gain antenna and the documented GPS C/N_0 acquisition threshold of 34 dB-Hz. All power levels, i.e., the noise power and the UWB power level will be referenced in a 20 MHz bandwidth for consistency. The UWB signal will then be added to this initial noise level and incrementally increased to the break lock level in a single channel of the GPS receiver. These measurements are currently scheduled to begin in early September.

2.3.3 RTCA SC159 Working Group 6 Discussion

The plan for assessing the potential UWB impact to Government radio systems other than GPS was presented at the June, 2000 meeting. No significant comments were received at that meeting; but at the August meeting the omission of Aeronautical Mobile Satellite (Route) Services (AMS(R)S) receivers from the candidate list was questioned. The response was that it was not on the list provided by FAA personnel of receivers likely to be susceptible to UWB interference.

The plan for assessing the potential UWB impact to GPS receivers was presented in August 2000 meeting and one comment was offered on the proposed test methodology. The NTIA plan proposes to incrementally add a composite noise and UWB signal until the receiver is forced to lose lock with the GPS satellite signal in the receiver channel of interest. At this point, the composite noise and UWB signal will initially be lowered by 2 dB and a reacquisition test will be performed. The comment was whether reacquisition can actually be accomplished within the manufacturer's performance specification at a level 2 dB below satellite break-lock. Additionally, it was suggested that even if the reacquisition is accomplished within the specified time, the GPS accuracy is likely to be degraded. The NTIA responded that the 2 dB back-off is but a starting point. If it is found that reacquisition cannot be accomplished at this point, then the composite noise and UWB signal will be further reduced (to a level 3 dB below break-lock) and the reacquisition test performed again. This process will be repeated until the point at which reacquisition can successfully be accomplished is reached. During this entire procedure, the receiver pseudo-range will be monitored and used to assess any degradation to the receiver accuracy.

2.4 UWB RFI Effects on L5 Receivers

The results from the test programs described in the previous sections deal basically with test plans and data to update L1 receiver RFI modeling. The RTCA study group has also been involved with L5 receiver modeling. Throughout the spring and summer of 1999 a theoretical RFI effects model was developed to support the RFI compatibility study for the new L5 frequency allocation. Since that time detailed computer simulations of the performance of the proposed "blanking" receiver implementation for reduced pulsed RFI susceptibility has shown the theoretical equations to be a reasonable first order prediction although conservative in some cases. Hardware testing has shown the possible limitations of analog mechanization of the blanker function. The interesting and significant UWB RFI data from Stanford suggest the real need to investigate the potential differences in L5 operation compared to L1.

3.0 RFI Encounter Scenario Development

3.1 Aviation Category I/II/III Precision Approach

3.1.1 Minimum RFI Separation Distance for Category I Approaches

In the study published in RTCA/DO-235 the Category I approach scenario was based on a mobile RFI source (MSS MET) at the height of the obstacle clearance surface on the extended runway centerline immediately under the 200 foot Cat I decision height point. The obstacle clearance surface defines a surface below which are all objects (including RFI sources) that would be physical obstacles to a safe approach. This complete surface is rather complex, but in the vicinity of the approach centerline it is an inclined plane whose slope for Category I precision approach operations is 1:34 beginning 200 ft in front of runway threshold. With appropriate assumptions for aircraft flight path deviation from the nominal 3° and for GPS antenna offset, the resulting antenna separation distance is 100 feet.

3.1.2 Minimum RFI Separation Distance for Category II Approaches

The RTCA study group is in the process of achieving consensus on the parameters for the Category II approach scenario. The following paragraphs contain a description of the Cat II approach problem and some discussion of options that documents the development to date.

The Category II precision approach obstacle clearance surface near the approach centerline has 1:50 slope (Figure 15). The 1:50 inclined plane begins 200 ft in front of runway threshold. At the Category II decision height (100 feet Height Above Threshold, HAT), the obstacle clearance surface is about 15.1 ft above the horizontal plane containing the extended runway centerline. At this point an object is permitted that is less than 15.1 ft. In fact the space under the surface can be filled with concrete right up to the obstacle clearance surface. Some obstacle clearance surfaces pass over state/interstate highways; in these cases the elevation of the highway may be lowered so that the traffic can pass under the surfaces. Obstacle clearance surfaces can pass over airport property or non-airport property.

The next step is to determine how close an aircraft on a Category II approach can get to the obstacle clearance surface where there could be an emitter causing RFI. The potential aircraft total system error (TSE) from the desired approach path is based on the Flight Technical Error (FTE) and Navigation System Error (NSE). The TSE distribution is obtained by computing the convolution integral using the truncated FTE and NSE distributions as described below.

Requirements for flight technical error (FTE) in the vicinity of the category II decision height are the FAA regulations for category II approval[8]. These regulations define a ± 12 ft vertical decision window on the pilot's indicator. The aircraft must be inside the window with a 95%

---

[8] FAA Advisory Circular 120-29,"Criteria for approving Category I and Category II Landing Minima for FAR 121 Operations," September 1970.

probability. If the aircraft is outside the window, the pilot does a "missed approach" maneuver (go-around). The window acts as a FTE tail-cutter that limits the vertical FTE flight path deviations to ±12 ft. *Note: Since many air carrier operations typically fly coupled approaches under VFR conditions, the Category II approach performance is typically achieved even when Category II weather minimums are not present.*

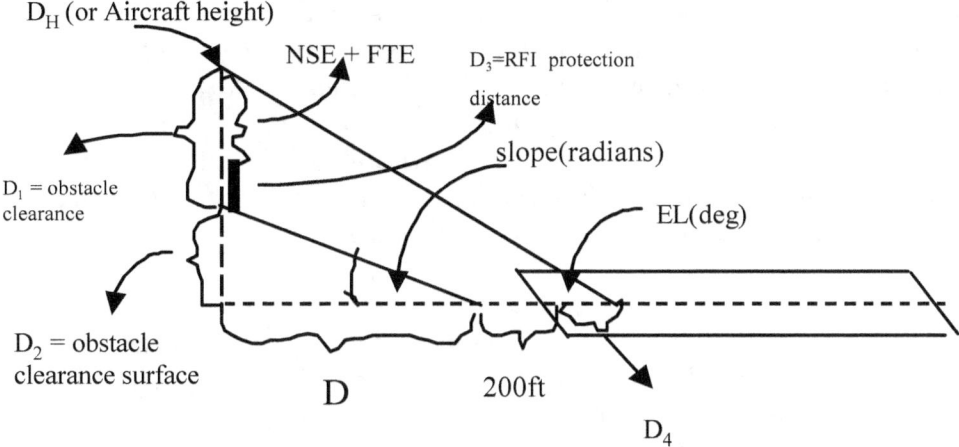

Aircraft antenna height above control point = 7ft

EL = 3 deg

D_H = 100 ft CAT II

D_4 = 50/tan(EL) ft

D = D_H/tan(EL) - D_4 - 200 = 754.1 ft for CAT II

slope = 1/50   for CAT II/III

D_2 = D*slope = 15.1 ft

Obstacle Clearance = D_1 = D_H - D_2 = 84.9 ft

aircraft antenna-to-obstacle surface = 84.9 + 7 = 91.9 ft

Figure 15 Category II Precision Approach Geometry

Pilots must maintain vertical course deviation within the Category II window which is half the full-scale deflection and where 0.7° is full-scale deflection. The conversion from degrees to feet for ILS is given by the following equation: $[0.7°\pi/180] \, 100/\text{Tan}(3°) = 23.3$ ft .The category II indicated window is ½ full scale or 23.3/2 = 11.65 ft ≈ 12ft. The pilot must do a go-around if he exceeds 1 dot for a 5-dot display (2 dots above the glide path and 2 dots below the glide path. For an 11- dot display there would be 5 dots above the glide path and 5 dots below the glide path so the pilot would do a go-around if the indictor exceeds 2.5 dots.

The 1σ NSE = 0.8m = 2.6 ft.[9]. For convenience the NSE distribution is truncated to a single-sided 5σ distribution, which is also the loss of continuity probability for fault-free errors. Thus, the 5σ NSE value is 13 ft.

*Note: A few minor considerations have not been included in the calculation. Although they will not significantly change the answer of 70 feet, we document them so that the US position will withstand the rigorous analysis of the ICAO panel. We need to consider the along track error coupling into a vertical positioning error (i.e., additional vertical error term = (the along track error) * tan GPA). This will be small term relative to the resulting minimum separation distance. Also we should calculate the absolute closest point that an emitter could be to the aircraft by taking the perpendicular distance from the obstacle clearance surface to the aircraft GPS antenna rather than just straight vertical. In other words take your vertical height answer times the cosine (1.1458 deg.) which is the angle of the 1/50 slope of the obstacle clearance surface.*

GPS LAAS loss of continuity due to RFI below 100 ft is generally not a concern because many aircraft follow an extended glide path that is generated by an interpolation from previous vertical measurements made by the landing system above 100 ft. This extended glide path is subsequently blended with vertical guidance derived from the aircraft's very accurate radar altimeter. In other words for many Category III implementations the LAAS vertical guidance may not be used below 100 ft and therefore the RFI is not a consideration in these cases.

Note: This assumption needs to be reviewed in the context of the overall requirements for Category III implementations and operations. In particular We should review the "blending" algorithms currently used to switch over to the radar altimeter in the vicinity of the prepared front course terrain (to accommodate the radar altimeter foot-print) about 450 ft before the 50ft Category III alert height.

The TSE distribution is based upon the FTE and NSE distributions. However in our case the FTE distribution is a truncated at 2σ because of the tail-cutter operation of the Category II window. This means that the TSE distribution function corresponding to the random variables FTE and NSE will not be Gaussian. (Recall that RFI event is always a loss of continuity event. Loss of integrity is not involved.)

The TSE distribution calculation involves the convolution of the truncated 2σ FTE distribution function with the truncated 5σ NSE distribution function using a fault-free loss-of-continuity probability of 2.87×10^{-7} (singled-sided) per 15s. For RFI considerations of ground-based mobile emitters we are only interested in the deviations below the glide path. The single-sided LAAS system continuity is 2×10^{-6} per 15s. Thus the assumed fault-free loss of continuity probability is about 10% of the LAAS system continuity[10].

The conclusion, the details of which are described below, is based upon the following calculations. The truncated FTE distribution function whose length for negative deviations is 12

[9]RTCA SC-159, "Minimum Aviation Standards for the Local Area Augmentation System (LAAS)," Doc. No. RTCA/DO-245 ,September 28, 1998, RTCA, Inc., Washington , DC
[10] RTCA/DO-245, ibid

ft is convolved with the truncated navigation system error (NSE) distribution function whose length for negative deviations is 13 ft. The result is a 5 σ total system error (TSE) of 21.9 ft with a fault-free loss of continuity probability of 2.87×10^{-7}.

The 5 σ TSE of 21.9 ft is associated with a 63 ft separation distance from the aircraft guidance reference point (GRP) to the closest point that an emitter could be located in the obstacle clearance region. Added to this distance is an assumption that the GPS antenna is more that 7 ft vertically above the GRP, which yields 70.0 ft of separation distance.

3.1.3 Category III Approach Scenario

The group has reviewed one proposal for a Category III scenario with essentially horizontal antenna separation. The RFI source is on a large aircraft waiting on the taxiway while another aircraft is over the runway threshold on approach. With the geometric constraints involved for proper Cat III operation, the overall path loss exceeded the necessary 76.1 dB even if the antenna gain toward the RFI source were only –5 dBic. The study group will continue to review available information to find other situations that may be limiting Cat III cases.

3.2 Other Aviation Scenarios

The following scenarios are planned for investigation by the study group to determine if any present a limiting case for receiver equipment or spectrum regulations.

Oceanic and enroute navigation: GPS is critical to improving the capacity of oceanic / remote airspace by allowing Air Traffic Service (ATS) providers to safely reduce the separation distances between aircraft. The greater precision of GPS enables providers to space aircraft from aircraft, rather than airspace to airspace. This eliminates the need to use vast blocks of airspace for enroute operations and allows for more accurate and flexible path paths. This further opens up more routes and operating environments as aircraft are no longer limited to flying within the broadcast constraints of terrestrial navigation systems. The resultant benefits are significant.

Non-precision approach: GPS with augmentation will enable precision approach operations for all properly equipped users under most scenarios. For non-FMS equipped aircraft, or for areas without adequate GPS coverage to meet all integrity, accuracy, availability, and continuity aeronautical safety requirements, GPS will provide improved timing and RNAV/VNAV (non-precision) approach guidance to the runway centerline.

Precision departure guidance: GPS will be used to improve traffic flow management at airports by allowing for precision departures that take advantage of the greater accuracy and flexibility of satellite navigation. GPS precision departures will enable curved and segmented departure paths around noise sensitive and other pertinent areas thus improving the capacity and flexibility of the terminal area without the continuous requirement for ATC radar vectoring.

Missed approach guidance: GPS will provide critical guidance to aircraft needing to execute a missed approach procedure near the ground in a terminal environment with potentially numerous other aircraft flying converging paths. Optimal functionality of such missed approach applications is based on key procedures that allow for reductions in terminal area obstacle/obstruction clearance areas based on the greater precision of satellite positioning.

Airport surface traffic management: GPS is a key enabler in providing greater situational awareness to all ground and air vehicles operating on an airfield. These positioning applications are intended to reduce incidents of inadvertent runway incursions and to expedite safe movement on the ground under all weather conditions. RTCA has published DO-247 on the role of GPS in surface operations that will like be the starting point for the scenario development.

Enhanced ground proximity warning system: The EGPWS is a terrain/obstruction sensor that is used by aircraft purely for safety-of-life applications, especially when the route of flight is in unfamiliar or hostile (mountainous) terrain. GPS data is integrated with moving map displays to provide the flight crew with the greatest situational awareness under these conditions. Lack of GPS information can lead to "map shifts" and other less safe or unreliable use of this equipment.

Automatic Dependent Surveillance (ADS) / Automatic Dependent Surveillance -Broadcast (ADS-B): ADS applications are based on the broadcast of GPS-derived position reporting to Air Traffic Service (ATS) providers, while ADS-B also sends this information out to nearby aircraft, similar to an "advanced TCAS" operation. ADS/ADS-B operations are crucial to evolving ATC procedures dependent on satellite navigation applications, as the safety and efficiency improvements of all other GPS applications are based on the ability of aircraft to reliably establish and share their position and intent information.

The scenarios described above could involve equally either L1 or L5 GPS. Another scenario that will be considered is the "transition-to-final approach fix" which applies to L5 only. In this scenario where DME density is high, the number of visible DME stations causing interference at L5 is diminishing to a point below the RFI threshold. The degree of interference needs to be determined to verify if planned mitigation strategy is sufficient.

3.3 Non-aviation Scenarios

Listed below (Table 5) are significant non-aviation applications (excerpted from the ITU-R WRC 2000 CPM Report[11]) for which scenario development should be at least considered. Given the long list, it seems likely the RTCA study group will have to focus on some key limiting cases. The group has had an introductory briefing from the US Coast Guard on the Vessel Traffic Service plans for an Automatic Identification System (AIS) based on GPS positioning and VHF Marine Band data link reporting. More discussion is scheduled for the group's September meeting. No information has been brought to the group yet from the public safety users other that the US Coast Guard.

National Geodetic Survey also presented information on RFI effects to GPS to the study group. The incidents occurred in the course of surveying aviation precision approaches for the FAA and seemed to involve cellular telephone and VHF 2-way radio interference.

---

[11] ITU-Radiocommunication Bureau, "Conference Preparatory Meeting Report On Technical, Operational And Regulatory/Procedural Matters To Be Considered By The 2000 World Radiocommunication Conference," Doc. No. CPM99-2/1-E, June 7, 1999, International Telecommunications Union, Geneva, Switzerland

Table 5. GPS Applications Candidates for Scenario Development

MARITIME and WATERWAYS	EMERGENCY RESPONSE
Navigation on the high seas.	Ambulance, police, and fire fighter dispatch.
Search and rescue.	Location for disabled vehicles and accidents
Harbour approach navigation.	**RAILROAD**
Vessel traffic services (ports and waterways)	Train control and collision avoidance
Dredging of harbours and waterways.	Railroad fleet monitoring
Positioning of buoys and marine nav aids.	Facility inventory control and management.
PUBLIC TRANSPORTATION	**LAW ENFORCEMENT**
Accident location reporting	Tracking and recovering stolen vehicles
Passenger and operator security monitoring	Tracking narcotics and contraband movements
Bus fleet on-the-road management	Maintaining security of high gov't officials while travelling
TELECOMMUNICATIONS	Border surveillance
Precise timing for messages	**ELECTRIC POWER**
PSTN network switch synchronization	Synchronization of frequency/phase
Cellular radiotelephone base station timebase	Fault event location
SURVEYING	**ENVIRONMENTAL PROTECTION**
National spatial data infrastructure	Hazardous waste site investigation
Precise aviation waypoint and landing aid locations	Precise location of stored hazardous materials

4.0 Summary and Further Work

Four UWB RFI effects test plans (Stanford, ARL:UT, and 2 from NTIA) were reviewed and the Stanford and NTIA plans were found generally similar and acceptable. There is some controversy, however, surrounding the ARL:UT plan. Compared with the other three plans, basic approach differences in the ARL:UT plan make it unclear if data from that plan can be directly compared with Stanford and NTIA data and if it can yield the necessary UWB noise equivalency factors.

Stanford preliminary test data has been reviewed and seems to indicate a potentially significant RFI effect for several UWB waveforms at present Part 15 limits. Considerable work remains to review the rest of the Stanford test data along with NTIA and other available data. Because of potential differences in GPS L5 receiver operation compared to L1, there is also a real need to investigate the UWB RFI effects on L5 receivers.

Scenario development is well underway for two key aviation cases. Consensus is building on a Category II precision approach case. More work is planned on other cases. Input and participation from users outside the aviation community are needed if meaningful non-aviation scenarios are to be developed.

The next interim report from the study group is scheduled for December 2000

www.ingramcontent.com/pod-product-compliance
Lightning Source LLC
Chambersburg PA
CBHW052027280526
45793CB00005B/1153